Ordinary Light:
A Correspondence

Laura Maher & L.I. Henley

LOS ANGELES † NEW YORK † LONDON † MELBOURNE

Ordinary Light: A Correspondence by Laura Maher & L.I. Henley

978-1-947240-70-4   Paperback

978-1-947240-71-1   eBook

Copyright © 2023 Laura Maher & L.I. Henley. All rights reserved.

First Printing 2023

Cover art by L.I. Henley

Layout and design by Mark Givens

For information:

Bamboo Dart Press

chapbooks@bamboodartpress.com

Bamboo Dart Press 033

www.pelekinesis.com

www.bamboodartpress.com

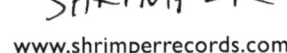
www.shrimperrecords.com

I can't tell one from another/ Did I find you or you find me?
—The Talking Heads,
"This Must Be The Place (Naive Melody)"

Table of Contents

LAURA MAHER

On Light and Leaving 7

Surfaces for Light 12

Call it Cloud 16

Nighttime Rituals 20

Love Stories 25

Bone 29

Dear Winter Light 34

Find Name, Road Home 39

Break 43

Swear 47

L.I. HENLEY

As good as any answer 10

From water to water 14

That sound follows light 18

Surrender 23

Memory/ blue currents 27

Lightness/ remains 32

Unknowingly/ winter evenings ... 37

New year poem 41

Music/ advice 45

Stay 49

Acknowledgments 52

About the Authors 53

It is an ordinary origin story of our time: the following poems grew from email exchanges, one phone call, a few text messages between writers living in adjacent deserts, the Sonoran and the Mojave. Yet, as we wrote to one another over a year, strangers before this correspondence and strangers still, we mapped a third space to think and to communicate, to write to an individual experience and dissolve what separates us.

On Light and Leaving, July

I like to take long walks at dusk, summer still
rising up from sidewalks, or where there are no sidewalks, dirt,
the street. I like to look into the light of my neighbor's windows,
not into their windows exactly, but the light from within.

The lights in my neighborhood burn as I like to think
my body does: not a thing in movement exactly, but the edge
of energy, possibility, warmth.

Light can do this.

It can make me think that my body does not
define me, does not
possess me, does not behave like a house I live in.
The light can be turned on or off. Can glow white or yellow, can show
the depth of a space. A room off a room off a room. A place
to throw a voice.

A light like an echo or a memory.

I like long walks, but when I write to you, I have to speak
to my poem to remember.
I say, *Poem, don't leave me. Poem, stay.*

Years ago, when I was sick and sure I wouldn't walk again,
I spoke to my body this way.
I said, *Body, don't leave me. Body, stay.*

Does a body know a thing before a mind has taught it?

At dusk tonight, the orange edge of a sunset could be seen
at the tree line, far off,
past the familiar slope of roofs, the angle like praying hands
beginning to come together, or like prayer itself.

The light can do this,
                         make me think about praying.

A plane left a sharp trail, the light a zipper to the evening sky.
I tried to get a picture for you, but an iPhone at dusk
does not see the light like I do.

Years ago, before I was very sick, before I knew anything
about bodies, my high school boyfriend and I drove
to the top of Campbell Avenue, to look at city lights and kiss.
    From far off, the lights looked
dangerous. Or it was these risks: the driving, the parking.

We sat on the hood of his parents' station wagon
and waited to get the nerve.

He had a small notebook
stored in the glove compartment to record the mileage
to every tank of gas.
I liked his hands reaching across, his hands catching in the light
pouring from the windshield, his hands reaching but not touching
my thighs, the lead scratch of pencil on paper.

How precious it can be to desire youth and maturity at once,
light and dark, touch and absence.
I said, *don't leave me*. It hasn't.

I wonder: do you pray? Find any usefulness in memories about your youth?

Do you see a light in the desert like a beacon or a warning?

It's summer now, and perhaps it always has been.
The light can do this.

Closer than my own body's hum, this light. The bats, called by dusk, their small bodies
cast against the sky, and all the while, I've walked beneath them, talking
to myself, the poem, saying: *don't forget.*

As good as any answer, July

We've never met, but I can see you,
can conjure you from a long stare
into campfire fed by greasewood,
this *you* walking in a desert
sister to my own, bats overhead
seen and unseen like webs, halos
around the moon, the bones of bats
not unlike those in our hands.
>*Does a body know a thing before*
>*the mind has taught it?*

For over a year, I couldn't walk
more than a few minutes at a time.
Standing was a chore.
I remember, once, abandoning
a full cart of groceries.
We were living in a resort town,
another desert. Jobless, we told our neighbors
we were retired. My partner would carry me
to the community pool
where I would swim with just my arms.
The water against my skin was painful.
Just the pressure of existence,
a weight that encompasses,
drowns a stone.
Even the white cotton sheets crushed
against me, everything heavy,

spackled with grit.
Surely my body asked to be taught what
the heat had done, what dazzling mirage
had taken shape, wind-spun and dizzy
on the salt flats. But what happens
when the mind loses the scent,
can't recover the tracks of the body,
or worse, sees the footprints gone
into the shimmer that looks so much like water?
Have you ever sunk yourself to the bottom
of a pool,   legs crossed,   eyes open,
just to let your breath right itself in globes of leaving light,
just to be sure a part of you still knows
which way is up?

Surfaces for Light, August

Learning to swim, I remember it was all directives:
    roll to your back
    find your float
    fill your belly with air and lift it to the sky—
my mother's voice, calming me:
if you find yourself in water, roll to your back and take deep breaths.

> Of course, there was fear. Sometimes a girl is taught to survive
> by being her most vulnerable. *If you find yourself in water.*

I see your body and its weight, its pain in water.
What a human thing, to be carried.

If you find yourself in water could be *if you find your body carried by*
    water—

> A nearly naked body of course, there was self-deprecation.

> There is this story of my childhood I like to tell:
> I was an eight-year-old breaststroke champion.

> This is mostly true:
> I won the city swim championships for my age that year. I
>   was eight.

> But this story is also a set-up for a joke: that *I peaked early*,
> which will draw a laugh and point away from the failure
> I often believe my body to be.

The truth is still: water is the only place I feel weightless and full
    of fear.

If you find yourself in water, find your way through it.

The child in me still swimming, her face turned to the sky, the sun—
a June afternoon—its promises and its punishments—

do you find yourself in water?
How do you make sense of your limbs, despite their weight—
how does your body find its float, its breath, its buoyancy?

My secret is that now
I'll only ever let myself swim at night, under the moon,
my body and the water just surfaces for the light to catch.

From water to water, August

In my desert, there are few true miracles.
Rarer still—a mind that knows water
from shimmer, root from lightning stone.
Here, a swimming pool is a marvel.
If you find one, you must shatter the cloudless
surface with your body, throw your bones
in the risk, dive into what might be
the world turned on its head.
I take it further still—try to find myself in water, ask
> *Am I down here? Are there pieces? Leaves and pennies,*
> *bracelets laced with plastic beads, little nightmares*
> *bathed in chlorine?*

Further still, past the place where doubt survives,
beyond the healthy suspicion that I am dreaming,
always dreaming when life is closest to answering itself,
when I am just about to partake
in the language of light.
Do you remember when language opened to you?
The unclouding, that cool brass key,
blue doors opening inward?
Would you believe me if I told you
I want to dive to a dark that terrifies,
swim into my second skin,
the vampire squid that fits me best?
When you find yourself in water.
When you find yourself at a lightless depth.

In the pool, my love and I would take turns
holding each other like a baby,
which means we took turns feeling strong
and needed. Or we took turns feeling that it was ok
to not be either. The water disorients. It turns us
upside down. It rights us in the end.
I want to tell you, poet, that you are still the champion,
that whenever you revisit the midnight zone
your body will know what to do—
make light, flashes and blips, the original language,
and I will watch   listen   send a message back.

Call it Cloud, September

Mirage, marvel, or pool: whatever it is there is
my own reflection ahead of me, dropping in, all legs,
then stomach, chest, arms, and face.

You say you want to dive to a dark that terrifies.
To me, this is
a way of saying memory, a well.

You ask if I remember when language opened to me
                 and I must confess: no.

My memories are both inhabited and moveable,
    beyond my grasp,
        something to hold in my body, to hold to my body,
like illuminating depth, the water you write of, like the cocoon
of your husband's arms.
These are held, tangible, yet indecipherable, charged.

A monsoon holds these:
a creosote top note, air thick with cicadic thrum and humidity,
the dusty smell of rain on dirt, the sluice of water
                down a saguaro, the slick limbs of the yucca.

So: maybe we have learned to love in the small, animal ways—

the shadows cast
    by words on a page, the sound of mesquite bean pods falling,
        our reflection in the surface of water.

I ask: where do you hold your memory?
What do you make of all these miracles?
You ask: *do you remember the unclouding?*   And I say: no, but
    monsoon. But monument. Mud adobe, brick and mortar.
Mountain, nightgown, revelation.

Call it   a flight of doves, a murder of crows,
a cast of hawks, a camp of bats.
Call it swamp cooler, shake and rattle, call it cicada,
chlorine, surprise, barrel cactus, deluge, call it family,
call it memory.

My grandmother used to say *all dressed up with nowhere to go*
    and I loved
  the song of this sentence, its sway and rhythm,
    its shimmy and sparkle.

  Language arrives and opens.

So: call it cloud, call it lightning storm, call it risk. I say
    postscript, I say promise.
I say: look at your reflection in the water and then,
    shatter its glass.

That sound follows light, September

It seems we inhabit the same spell
of thunderstorms, careen somewhere between
burst and break, run for cover
in the suddenness of rainfall, and in the pause
try to conjure a new deluge.
Sometimes the gathering of molecules
is enough. I know it's true because
when you said, *the sound of mesquite
bean pods falling*, I landed lightly in my chair,
not knowing I'd been hovering,
lightly as when I was a seed,
papery small, an eyelash caught on the cloak
of infinity. Yet here I am with my billions of cells,
the lightest of sleepers, every whisper from every
unusual cloud unfurling me from the tuck of dark.
I am wakeful, still reeling from the act of being born,
the miracle (or were there several?)
of growing limbs, two hands to cover my face,
toes to suck in my simple mouth.
That cells harden for our benefit,
ossify into spinal cord, uncurl us from our tunneled gaze—
know what I mean?
It's enough to keep me sleepless until the day I die.

And, friend—can I call you that?—I don't believe death
will be any kind of miracle,

just a wrestling match that wears me out,
then further out, all the way out.
There's no sorrow in this, though I'm awake
and at my window again.

Does this ever happen to you?
> A too late meal, the dog snoring triumphantly,
> then those dream particles tremble the air,
> clot and rise,
> walk about the room? Semi-lucidness,
> lightning's ghostly tributaries,
> counting one Mississippi, two…

I need to know: do you have trouble sleeping
when the moon is full and blankets the boulders
or is it the sliver that divides the dark,
makes you restless?

And does it ever hit you sideways,
your hand having never been inside
my own in the customary grasp?
Hello, so nice to finally meet you. And yet…
What is distance, what is separate, when two people
can share a memory, cup rain
from the same ruptured cumulus,
find quartz and lost shoes in the same dry wash,
say monsoon and hear the peal, the sound and the light,
one following the other,
never more than seconds apart?

Nighttime Rituals, October

This is the third night of lightning storms without the relief of rain.

When I stepped outside one last time before bed, the sky
was electric with the mottled light of heat lightning
and the air smelled of a distant brushfire.

There is the risk within the beauty.
Something in my desire to approach an edge while holding my
    hand back to a steadying branch.

Tonight, my dog is displeased with the lightning.
I find her curled in the closet behind my hamper and strewn shoes.

She mistakes the thunder for voices, and there's nothing
that calms her, except
    to say *sweet girl*   *sweet girl*   *sweet girl.*

Maybe, like you, I am tired and wish for sleep but know it won't
    come.

The seed of your body could also be the seed
of mine, that we grew to be
the limbed creatures we are under the shade
of desert trees, mica flakes in our hair,
creosote perfuming our skin.

Let's not mistake the shade of a desert tree for anything than what
    it really is:
        a place to build an altar,

a place to pray,
a place to bury your dead and bury your dreams,
so the former will find peace and the latter will find a safe
place to grow.

A desert tree's worst sin is that it's rooted
but I've loved the low, horizontal arms of a mesquite,
the green, knobbed limbs of a palo verde,
the stripped bark of a cottonwood.

These are enough

to sustain, which is what we all want when we have a restless heart.
Is your heart as restless as mine?

Yesterday, I read a translated poem that used the word *beast*, but
had a parenthetical note
revealing that the translator wished to have used the word *animal*.

It seemed to him that *animal* would be nearer to the poet's
original desires, but *beast* fell more heavily on the tongue,
sounded blunt
and mean, which were stronger desires of the poet.

On nights when I cannot sleep, I wish not to be an animal
or a tree, but to be a translator's note—
something understood, something to inspire wonder.

I say *sweet girl*   *sweet girl*   *sweet girl* like a bedtime prayer.

Is your heart as restless as mine? Does your voice in the empty
house still startle and surprise?

And what of that hand reaching for a steadying branch? *Hello,*
    sweet friend.

There is something about sweetness or a voice in the dark.
Yes, friend—call me friend—the edge
    feels nearest during long summer midnights, I know.

But that sound, that light—how one can be both *crack* and *strike*
    at the same time.
The desert's language writes in ways we must translate, and we
    can be ready at a blank page.

Surrender, October

I write to you from a state of fire:
a geography keen to combust like a feather stick.
All this while Mars is closest, and the longest
Total lunar eclipse gifts us a blood moon.
Do you think this conflagration will purify? Instruct?
Wake the herald of a fifth season?
All I know is that ash falls with such ordinary lightness
I almost stick out my tongue, welcome it like snow.

So much beauty acts as kindling:
dead branches,
lace curtains,
love notes inked in cursive,
pine needles,
frayed rope,
the lathe—its nest of shavings.

I saw a photo in the paper of the exact moment
a woman in a gas mask found her engagement ring
in the wreckage and knew that love stories
begin and end the same way. The look of astonishment,
then recognition, not so different as when
she first saw the ring in a silk-lined box,
which reminds me that I keep finding the same
slough of snakeskin in my yard,
thinking briefly each time that it's new, my breath

stopped by its cathedralness, pulled inside
the hall of paper windows.
When I see it, I have to call out *snakeskin*
a steadying branch, name its passivity,
windblown lace, the gentleness of having *been* here
and not *being* here.

Snakeskin. What's more instructive of letting go?
The eyes go milky, blind,
the beast retreats.
Here is the animal most vulnerable.
Here the body frees itself from itself.
I want to fully trust this offering of beauty. All this change.
Beast or animal, diamond in the wrack,
paper cathedral, hallowed fever.

Love Stories, October

My first cursive letters were an incantation:

letters connected by threads, words built by my hand
to unlock adult secrets.

My cursive letters were a thing I possessed singularly.

I wrote secret thoughts on scraps of paper and buried them
in the undeveloped desert behind my childhood home.

It is such an ordinary thing to love.

Such an ordinary thing to practice singular love, steal it away
from others, to practice sweetness to yourself but hide it.

***

Last year, the man I loved tattooed a coyote on his chest.
I loved to run my hands over the darkened lines of its fur,
its ears, its eyes. My love for him, a wild animal.

The loss of him, another beast, another body
to unlearn, a secret to write and bury.

The scream you practiced but then cannot command.

I swear, the wind here sometimes sounds like the sheets
    of my lover's bed.

***

What I know: a desert is vast

but you can learn it.

The problem of my childhood incantations
was that I forgot the buried places as soon as I covered them.
The magic I learned held its mysteries as much as its revelations.

A desert is vast

and the in-between place for stories, places to learn lessons.

I swear, the wind here sometimes sounds like the voice of my
    grandmother,
calling to me sweetly down a long hallway.

What secrets of adulthood have I unlocked?

My hands were always stained with soil or ink, I can't remember.

Memory/ blue currents, October

A desert is vast, as you say,
and surely, we weren't the only girls
who buried our words in the sand dunes,
dry lake beds. Probably I dropped
a few into mineshafts. I still dream about
not having anything to wear to school dances—
a closet full of outfits shaped like deflated balloons
or spent condoms, a bra made
of lettuce cups, one dress that looks promising
until it's on me, and I feel it melting off
like warm lard. Always the dance has begun,
everyone has arrived but me.
Do I even need to tell you
I was a lonely girl? That even now
when I have more than my fair share of love,
still, I want some of yours?
The story of a tattoo on a man's chest,
the darkened fur, the eyes of a coyote,
and I'll bet the mouth
was open, howling, calling out.
When you shared your secret with me,
I dug up all the love letters I buried
in the Mojave, kissed the chests of every man
I've loved and left. Forgive me: I'm the greediest bird
with the longest beak. Maybe it's because
my house was so far away from the town,

the school, the people.
And because I loved dancing so much,
and because all the things I loved
seemed to float away on their own blue currents.
Or these are not my memories at all.
Maybe I dug up one of yours
or that of another woman who was once a lonely girl.
The *not having* follows us into the *having*.
The absence of sweetness stays on the tongue.
I have plenty of clothes now, but the dances
are over. If you were here, I'd put on a record,
and we'd push the furniture onto the patio.
I'd show you the moves I've been practicing for years
and years. We'd try to dance our bodies into
the present moment where the love is—
do you think we could do it? Our hands in soil,
our faces smeared with ink.

Bone, December

This letter has taken me a month—
more, if I count the days like burned matchsticks.
Days can feel like fires I've made then extinguished.
You were not far from my mind, though I know I never said.

***

I moved houses, did I say? Living alone can make time

feel stretched out, empty, and also perfectly contained.

My new house has Saltillo tile and a huge eucalyptus tree that
    sheds fat leaves
and long strips of bark in the yard.

When wind rolls through its limbs, forty feet above my bed, it
    sounds like rushing water.
How do I explain that I feel purified?

***

    Friend,

you have never taken what wasn't offered.

Last month, I found a bleached-white bone of some animal's
    spine in an arroyo
and I wished that you had been there to hold it with me.

A back bone—stripped of anything that made it once alive—
is lighter than understanding.

I couldn't know—by vulture, water, time—what took the skin,
    fur, sinew.
I couldn't know by what means it was carried and dropped there—

just that it arrived.

You'll know that my impulse was to put it in my pocket,

    to remove it from a resting place,
and then it was to bury it, to secret it away.

Last month, there was more news about detained children,
stories about how we will be voting
and a televised discussion of sexual assault on the Senate floor
    (again).

More gun violence.

I do not know how art saves.

How will art save? What humanity can be found by my hands?

    ***

Last month I wrote:

after a fire, we exist in memory as much as in dream

I think this was meant for you, so I'll send it now on a scrap of paper,
    more kindling than anything else.

***

Did I tell you he called me *sugar*? My old love?
I wonder: where does the sweetness we've known go
                          except to settle into bone?

Lightness/ remains, December

In the last vestige of daylight, I stand looking at sky,
sight on the pitch of a hawk before the swoop—
neck strained, appearing as a woman lost,
which is sometimes true, and question
how many words there are for *twilight*.
Not enough. I must tell you that waiting
is my best teacher, that it humbles me.
Folds me gently to my knees
then flat on the earth where I'm obliged
to smell the grass seeds waking.
The flood from two weeks ago.
And now a carpet of soft, short, patchy grass,
green even in its dying.

I want to see your house, want to know
if you walk barefoot on the Saltillo tile,
if you ever look out your kitchen window,
washing dishes, arguing with your own hands
what should have been said,
and mistake the tree bark for roosting doves.
Happens to me all the time.

That bone, it must've been incredibly light,
so much that you wanted someone there
to hold it with you and say,
Yes, there is the slightest heft here—existence.
In the palm of an unfeeling world,

I think we have both felt so imperceptibly light before.

I believe that my word could be a dove's
dropped seed, and your nerves would alight.
Is this how art saves?
For this, I would wait and wait and wait.
I would stare down the gloaming, travel through
the tiny doors of dried bone.
I don't want to give my words to anyone with less a feeling.
I don't want to be misread,
the spinal column of a small being unloved.

I swear the country is bound in cellophane right now,
each nerve individually wrapped.
A hardness. Sugar into bone as you say.

My college students do not believe Democracy is real.
They say, "fake news."
Still, I have to love them, swallow despair,
re-explain comma rules,
read them poetry in between the headlines.
What did my mother used to do? An apple core
in the brown sugar to keep it soft.
Something about forgiveness, something about baking
even if you can't eat,
your stomach in knots, the violent hues
of the election map,
ticker tape below, stepping out to catch
the pink rim of sunset,
conjure up new words for what remains.

Dear Winter Light, December

The daylight is sunk by the time I leave my office. These are lonely hours,
the ones hidden between leaving one place and getting to the next.

And the time spent forging my body to be
                              as lithe as a beam of light—
this, too,
was waiting, was conjuring, was creation.
How little I knew of the properties of sunlight, chasing it as I did.

***

How do I write about my country's fears about the world?

Dear Country,
        Dear World,

Dear Lines on a Map,   or Dear Friend—

Can you imagine? There was once a person who decided that all blue lines on a map meant *river*.

Tonight, blue light from my computer screen:

      river.

***

We share rivers, your desert and mine.

We could stand on the same winter rye grass
watered by the river.

We could stand and wait to be healed.

In sun or in water, we'd learn the song of someone's god.

Do you think that fear came before language?
    That it rose in the throat and met the shock of air, made its
        guttural expression?
                Or was the first word *tenderness*? The soft hollow
                      below the beloved's lip?

***

Let me tell you: the years I spent waiting for someone else
to say *You are a beautiful, lithe beam of light* were not wasted.

I learned to write into it, cast spells to it, become light and stone.

***

Your hands at the kitchen sink, making doves from soap bubbles.

***

Dear Sunlight, Dear Winter Light,

Dear Body as Light, Body as Stone,

These are hours to learn: beauty and brutalness alike,

the tenderness of the personal pronoun   *my country*
    my heartbreak.

Unknowingly/ winter evenings, December

If you asked me how to get to my house,
I couldn't tell you the names of the roads
even though I've traversed them since sixteen.
The names won't stick. Or I know them but
can't put them in order. I could hand you a bouquet
of dark roads, no streetlights but plenty of thorns:
this one is Jupiter, is Old Woman, is Baby's Breath.
That last one isn't a road, at least not here.
There are nights, more often than I'd like to admit,
where for several moments I think I'm lost.
Wendell Berry said, "To know the dark, go dark."
So, I tell myself I can drive all night
in this uncertainty. At least until the tank is empty.
Then I'll have to strip naked, enter the river.

This is where I should tell you about my fears.
What I was doing before careening slick straits
of winter road and writing this poem
in my head—teaching an adult education class
in Twentynine Palms, my classroom
down the hall from the cyber security class
where fourteen-year-olds learn to make drones,
the child development class where girls cradle
realistic babies in their bony arms.
Babies cry, drones buzz. My students are
all women with children. They come when
they can. We have to go back to the beginning

every week, go back to nouns—concrete,
countable things we can see and touch
(babies, drones). What we have in common:
we are all *desert women*. We have brown sunspots
and thin, tousled hair. We know what it takes
to clear a mound of tumbleweeds blocking
a gate. We know where the river is,
but we don't go near it, for there are mouths to feed.
I don't say anything when one woman excuses
herself while I'm talking prepositions,
comes back smelling of whiskey.
That was at eleven this morning—much too early
for *under, over, beneath*, the wind knocking us down,
our tree-legs righting us again.

I fear I'm a total fraud, telling women
prepositions are essential for giving
directions when no one gives
directions anymore. For telling them it's ok
to be lost, to not know, to move ahead with feeling.

Dear Very Young Country, what will you be
when you grow up? My sweet one,
can you imagine a future?
You are beautiful when you sleep,

but you can't sleep all day.

I drive slowly, reading all the street signs,
expecting always for a stray dog or
lean coyote to dash unknowingly across.

Find Name, Road Home, December

What I read as *fear* others read as *common sense*, what I read as *broken* others read as *rusty*.

Abandon can be equal parts *expulsion* and *release*, *tremor* and *quiet*.

In a desert town, a woman must know that despite her own quiet, some part of her day has been tracked:

coyote // mountain lion // border patrol // man in store // man in car // Google // Apple

I knew this woman who came to town to preserve a historical downtown building.
For weeks, she scrubbed paint from baked clay tiles with a toothbrush.
The building, restored to beauty, scrubbed clean and shining, clay tiles in yellow and black art deco, now sits vacant,
crumbling in a new way.

Who will scrape the gum from the sidewalks
now that the woman has gone?

There's something about desert towns that implies *leaving* or *left*.

How do you teach your students to conjugate verbs when they only know their embodiment?
All the roads lead back to home with Google Maps, or another equivalent.

With or without my phone, if I have taken myself somewhere
    once, I can find my way back.

It is an unusual skill, one I shared
with my grandmother—a woman who could find
her way through cotton field and cemetery, through classroom
    and chicken coop.
What did she know of fear?

And where do I begin when,   if in my telling of these women,
    I flatten them like a paper map?

The woman who walks by a river is said to cry for the children
    she drowned.
And we are taught to walk in the children's footpath—
feel the fear of the mother.

And what of the mother's fear?
Who walks in the footpath of a woman's shame? Sadness?

Walking or driving   the crunch of sand underfoot like
    hard edges of consonants

like *enter*   or *walk*   *drive*

want want want

In daylight, does Google find you as it does for me, name your
    home *home*?

New year poem, January

Are we beyond imagining now?
You've just had a birthday and mine is waving
to me from that dry hill, or it's a white
windmill turning without me. I can't tell.
I'm dying my hair now
and taking pills to replace the work
my thyroid once did. I have an entire cabinet
dedicated to vitamins. I can't say I've lost
strength, or that I'm any less in love.

Some days I am the building you speak of,
restored, scrubbed clean and shining by the years,
by the meteors that graze, the giant birds
that pluck my finery. Others, I am the baked clay,
the soiled toothbrush, sidewalk, any knowable
object, purpose-lead, but also the gone woman,
her last sigh before she left.

The New Year always arrives like a drug, or like
a seductress neither male nor female,
legs spread, and I want the void of it,
want to slip into my own halo.
I could have sworn I wrote a letter telling you
we should both start walking and meet halfway.
That I know your good senses will bring you
to me even if I'm stuck in a cactus forest
in a state neither of us can claim.

Even if I walk due east into the sun
and reach a dried-up dam instead of the parted
lips I thought the year would be, I think
your hand would touch my shoulder, I think
poetry would save me. Last night in the tub,

I read a micro-memoir piece in which the author
kissed the parted lips of her newborn baby.
It was a list of the best kisses of her life.
She said it was a *soul-kiss*, and I felt the water turn cold.
Is grace not wanting what you don't have?
Is it the act of cupping sadness in a nest
of your own making, of softening the landing?
I thought by now I would know
so much more, but here I am with more grace
than knowledge, a lace curtain swishing
behind a stack of half-read books.
I'm walking to meet you halfway, friend,
and when I see you, I'm going to ask you
what it means to be a woman,
and do you think I should try again,
and do you hear in my voice the children
and the good ideas I've given to the river,
and would you like some cake?

Break, January

Here: I wonder what advice I have to give about navigating
the passage of one year to the next, of shedding expectations

like shedding a robe before the floor of the bathtub. Yes: I find
the weight of the robe on my shoulders rarely matches

its soft drop to the floor. It carries, instead, like
a whisper or a kiss. I, too, just know the parted lips of my lover,

the parted lips of where the desert meets water, the parted valleys
of my life *before* and *after*. Each pause contains what was

and what won't be, but I find so rarely does it offer
more than the relaxed slope

of a body sliding into water, a letter sent to a friend,
one year floating to the next. I spent the last night

of the year eating date cake with candied blood orange—
a coincidence noted and as easily devoured.

What I know if this year, just one day in: we can divide
our lives in myriad ways, divide

our bodies by what is well and whole
or what is lacking and sick, draw a line between desire

and longing. What I also know: tear gas can be launched
across a border because divisions are fluid and made.

My friend delivered her daughter three days
before the end of the year, and as I waited to hear from her I felt

suspended in the water-gone-cold moment,
the closest to frightened joy as I can touch.

I've long divided my desires into worthy and unworthy.
a more convenient sorting for my mind than my soul. A *soul-kiss*,

she said. Have you made a list of the best kisses of your life?
What does it mean if I haven't sorted any of the fleeting kisses?

Did I tell you that my desire
was always that I'd be a mother?

Or that now, finding myself childless, this desire has little to do
with my age and more to do with how much I love to take long walks

and study the night sky?
Dropped into the river, time is less a thrown rock

and more a cup of sand, emptied little by little.
Will you—next month, when you've crossed the white hill,

when you've learned the early lessons of the year, when we've found
each other somewhere halfway between—

will you tell me your advice? I'd love to share some cake.
I still consider it one of the worthiest of desires.

Music/ advice, February

I think the best advice I ever got
came from music, how to really feel it
when you've been wronged,
how to slow dance with your heartache,
tune your longing like a trumpet.
The music said, *You can stop feeling this
anytime you want. But why would you want to?*
The sadness had a warmth, like a stove,
and I pressed my hips to it.
Would you believe me if I told you
that even now, married to my truest love,
I sometimes miss that music?
Did you know I sometimes sing?
Blues, mostly. I like it slow like that,
predictable in rhyme and bottomless
in grief. "I go out walking, after midnight,
out in the moonlight…searching for you…"
The weeping willow kills me every time.
One time I played the role of a wife
pushed to the edge
and died from pills on an outdoor stage
while Patsy Cline sang.
I can't remember why the wife
was depressed, but I'll never forget
the long-leg spiders all over my body
as I lay there dead.

I was sixteen and had my first on-stage
kiss and death all in the same night.
Isn't that what all girls want—
the night-hushed drama of it?
Do you sing? Do you sing when you
go out walking under the night sky?
I pretended the crawling, the tickle,
was fuzzy light coming down from the stars.
The stars are very close tonight, I told myself.
The stars are very bright.
My high school boyfriend had driven
all the way to Idyllwild to watch the play
on opening night. I was ready to break up with him,
loving the end as much as the beginning,
wanting that good music warm in my hips,
and kissed the boy on stage (my play husband)
extra-long. Then I died with a dramatic stagger,
a prolonged, silent gape, my mouth an O
that sang out Os above the heads
of the audience. That was twenty years ago.

I want more kisses, more birthdays, more life.
Still, it was a good, dreamy death—
the best I've ever had—with spiders and stars
and people watching. My Os floating off into the pines.

Swear, February

What warmth we have known, turning our cheeks to rest on hot
    sand,
soaking up sunshine through skin, flushing with desire—for life,
    or a kiss, for a poem—

or catching spring winds by our hair.

A heat like this—I know it. A heat like this, warmth
like I could consume it.

You say—*the sadness had a warmth*—we know how sadness can be
    a comfort has much as it can scald.

I wonder:
    can my memory of something hot
    work as well to prevent a burn, the shock of it blooming
    as easily, as early as spring poppies flush the mountains
    in gold, in yellow?

These, named California poppies, were blown by warming winds too.

With winter shorter and stranger every year, I return
to all the ways that a human body can scar or mend,
can want or create.

Though I will plant my legs firmly into the earth, this tells me

that this desert is rare, its frailty its strength.
                                I look at the mountains,

or hear soft Os drifting from California, and I know just as well that

there's as much magic as there is science in every transition, I swear.
If I could leave my skin, my body, would I?

Stay, April

It's spring already and I never told you
about the late February snow—
waking to it, the silence, the world finally
turned right side up, lungs emptied.
The snow was a hushed choir.
Even the crows bowed their heads
on the power line. My boots crunching,
knees wading into reverie.
The backyard a forgotten moon,
and I without a radio—no home
to report to. Walking wasn't the same,
my vision blurred, and I knew I was a visitor again.
I've been meaning to ask you:
what did you discover, what rose to the surface,
when you were ill for so long, when you lost
the ability to walk?
My diary in 2012: *Went to the pool today. I had to be carried.*
Drank Tequila from a plastic cup and my spine grew hot.
Illness, like heat, uncovers, displaces,
shines a light, stirs what's long been dead.
In the snow, the quiet bloomed for miles.
I was sure I could hear you turn
the page of a book. Could hear the lightness
of your being over the hushed choir,
the crows tuning their teardrop
heads to your frequency. I waved to you

from my drifting moon, and knew
that Arizona, like California, like America,
is not a place, but an idea.
The snow is long gone. The flowers do not
apologize for their beauty, taking over
Chollas and other cactus, invading dead scrub brush,
carpeting the deep-cut washes.
The heat has a sadness. We are coming to an end.
The final act of blazing stars, Canterbury bells, asters.
I want to say something that will make you stay.
If I could leave my skin, I wouldn't.
I want to see how it ends, what the heat does,
how long the papery ears of globemallow will last.
Time is no one's friend—short winter, early spring.
Poem, don't leave me. Poem, stay.

Acknowledgments

Exposition Review: "On Light and Leaving," "As good as any answer"
Juked: "Love stories," "Memories/ blue current," "Bone," "Lightness/ remains"
Oyster Pages: "Swear," "Music/ advice"
Superstition Review: "Surfaces for Light," "From water to water," "Call it Cloud," "That sound follows light"
The Hunger: "Surrender," "Dear Winter Light"
Watershed Review: "Unknowingly, winter evenings," "Find Name, Road Home"

About the Authors

Laura Maher is the author of the chapbook, *Sleep Water* (Dancing Girl Press, 2017). Her poetry and prose has appeared in *Quarter After Eight, The Common, Crazyhorse, The Collagist, New Ohio Review*, and *Third Coast*. Laura holds a Bachelor of Arts from the University of Arizona, a Master of Arts from the University of Texas at Austin, and a Master of Fine Arts from Warren Wilson College. She lives, works, and writes in Tucson, Arizona.

Find her at lauramaher.com.

L.I. Henley hails from the Mojave Desert of California. An artist and writer, her books include *Starshine Road* (Perugia Press Prize, 2017) and the novella-in-verse, *Whole Night Through*. Her art, poetry, and prose have appeared most recently in *Adroit, Brevity, The Indianapolis Review, Calyx, The Bellingham Review*, and *The Los Angeles Review*. Her personal essays have been awarded the *Arts & Letters*/Susan Atefat Prize and the *Cincinnati Review*'s Robert and Adele Schiff Award.

Visit her at www.lihenley.com.

112 N. Harvard Ave. #65
Claremont, CA 91711

chapbooks@bamboodartpress.com
www.bamboodartpress.com

www.ingramcontent.com/pod-product-compliance
Lightning Source LLC
Chambersburg PA
CBHW080943040426
42444CB00015B/3425